Praise for

A Recipe for Biblical Success Workbook

One thing you can always expect from Jason Coache is transparency. In this book he openly shares his frustrating experience as a person driven to be "successful." The other thing that I've come to expect from Jason is that he learns from his mistakes and grows from what he learns. This book is some of the wonderful fruit of that growth. If you are a driven person, his teaching can help you avoid hitting a hard dead end on your road to success. The biblical instruction in these pages will be life-changing for some.
—**Dr. David A. Ridder**, Senior Pastor, Bayside Chapel

***

A Recipe for Biblical Success is a much-needed book. Far too many Church Leaders are defining ministry in the wrong way. Jason, with careful insight and practical experience, gives us a plan for how to make ministry about serving God. This is a book I'll be giving to Pastors and Leaders I coach and mentor.
—**Paul Johnson**, Past Executive Vice President of Converge Worldwide and Pastor of Woodridge Church

***

It has been a joy to see Jason harness his God-given ambition through the joys and sorrows of life and ministry. He has lived the wisdom in this book. This is invaluable insight for weary travelers and wounded faith workers that will help reframe your vision and recapture your first love.
—**Andy Needham**, Regional VP, Converge Northeast

***

In a culture that highly values success, we can mistakenly adopt worldly perspectives and measures for success. When this happens, we may lose our true sense of purpose, misplace our values, and even lose ourselves and our families. Jason reminds us of the importance of returning to a biblical definition and measure of success, namely, "Biblical success is when God's heart and God's ways become my heart and my way." In this practical and helpful guide, Jason draws upon his own experience and demonstrates how the truth of the Word of God helps us to return to God's perspective on success and allows us to regain our true purpose. This inspiring and helpful book is much needed in our post-Covid ministry world.
—**Dr. Matt McAlack**, Director of Youth & Family Ministry Programs, Cairn University

***

As a "successful" business owner for over 35 years and now the President of an International Non-Profit serving Malawi, Africa - I wish I had this book when I first started. Defining success is something we always struggled with as a Christian-Operated Business. Jason does a masterful job in providing the proper perspective - biblical! His transparency and authenticity illuminates and softens the hard truths shared within this book. A must read for those who want to redefine and challenge themselves on what success looks like in both their personal and professional lives.
—**Steven Chartier**, President, Good Soil Partners

***

In this book Jason Coache shows the immense benefit of doing the hard work of self-reflection. His words are challenging. Through his own experiences, he shows that God sets a standard for our lives that is much different that we naturally assume. God's way is truly the better way, but it will require from us a changed mindset and dedicated effort in a heavenly direction. The chapters contain several powerful descriptions that will make you stop and think introspectively.
—**Brian Weber**, Regional President & Executive Minister, Converge Midatlantic

***

Authentic and helpful are the two words that come to mind after reading, *A Recipe for Biblical Success*. Jason's willingness to share his own journey is helpful and enlightening. Too often, we have traded what is really important to follow the dream of success the way the world defines it. Jason helps us identify the folly that comes from chasing the world and to rewrite the definition of true ministry, family, and leadership success.
—**Lee Stephenson**, Senior Pastor, Harvest Community Church

A Recipe For Biblical Success Workbook

A Guide to Honor God in the Pursuit of a Successful Life

Jason Coache

Published by KHARIS PUBLISHING, imprint of KHARIS MEDIA LLC.

ISBN-13: 978-1-63746-192-1

ISBN-10: 1-63746-192-5

Library of Congress Control Number: 2022948624

All KHARIS PUBLISHING products are available at special quantity discounts for bulk purchase for sales promotions, premiums, fund-raising, and educational needs. For details, contact:

Kharis Media LLC

Tel: 1-479-599-8657
support@kharispublishing.com
www.kharispublishing.com

How the workbook is designed:

This workbook is designed to help bring the reader to a point of action. From the introduction to the conclusion, and every chapter in between, a list of reflection questions is given to the reader. These questions start with reading reflections and then onto deeper study questions. These two sections are meant to drive the understanding of general concepts found within the section being highlighted within the book. From here we move to personal reflections and finally a challenge. This is meant to bring you to a point of action. "I've grown in understanding, I've thought about it in my life, now what?" The challenge is meant to be that one final action step. For a challenge to be a challenge, it must be, catch this, *challenging*. This is not meant to be easy, this is meant to push you.

This is prayed over:

My prayer is that this workbook is what will bring the whole project to life. I pray that here is where we begin to see life change. My prayer is that this is where the truths are found, first and foremost, the Word of God, becomes truth in your life. This is my prayer for you, even as you continue to walk this journey. I want to see you, as driven as you are, driven to honor God in your relentless pursuit of the King. As I have prayed for the reader, know that as you read this, you are prayed for.

TABLE OF CONTENTS

INTRODUCTION

Reflection Questions

What is your understanding of success going into this book?

What is your reaction to this quote from the introduction? *"I have heard it said in church planting circles that "healthy things grow." Yet, growth isn't always a measure of success. It is simply a measure. I grew by 20 pounds during Covid. That wasn't success, that was sin."*

What is your reaction to this quote from the introduction? *"So what is biblical success? It's not a big house when our Savior died homeless. It's not more books when our Savior didn't write a book. It's not winning a popularity contest when the crowd helped put our Savior to death. If we have the world's metrics for success, then at some level, we will have to do things in the world's ways to achieve their metrics."*

As the book unfolds, we will unpack this definition: *Biblical success is when God's heart and God's ways become my heart and my way.* What is your initial reaction to this definition?

What makes the recipe "biblical" and how is it different from the world's recipe?

Deeper Study Questions

In the introduction, we survey Proverbs 3:3-4. Let's look at the context. Read Proverbs 3:1-2. How does this help you with your understanding of Proverbs 3:3-4 and our discussion on success?

Now read Proverbs 3:5-8. You have likely heard these verses before. How does this help you with your understanding of Proverbs 3:3-4 and our discussion on success?

Read Matthew 7:21-23. The person described here seems, on paper, like a successful Christian. Why would we naturally say this seems successful? Why doesn't God see it as successful?

How does our verse (Proverbs 3:3-4) and our definition of success, help us understand this Matthew 7 passage?

Personal Reflections

What ingredients (steadfast love, commitment, faithfulness, and heart) most challenge you as you think of a successful Christian life?

How did the discussion of favor challenge your preconceived notions on this word?

At the moment, in which area of your life (to be honest with yourself) does God not see as successful? Why?

What does God's definition of success look like in that area?

Challenge

Having identified an area of growth (an area that is not currently successful in God's eyes) and having identified how success looks like in this area, my challenge to you is to bring immediate action towards success in that given area. To help, use the queues below:

Define the problem. What really is the problem I am dealing with in this area?

> Be specific. If your weight is an issue, look up healthy BMI, then get on the scale and say, "I am 46 pounds overweight." If it is giving, look up your previous years' giving, determine what percentage you gave, and say, "Last year, I gave 1.6% to the church, I need to raise my giving by 8.4%." If you don't feel like you are a good spouse, be bold right now and ask your spouse, "how could I be a better husband/wife to you?" Then come back here and name the problem!

In one year, what would it look like for you to be successful in this area?

What are three things you can positively change and do over the next 30 days to help you towards that one-year goal?

Who can hold you accountable for these action steps? (REACH OUT TO THEM)

What could possibly keep you from accomplishing these goals? What will you do about it?

Conclude your time praying over the action steps you will be taking.

Notes

INGREDIENT #1: STEADFAST LOVE

"Let not steadfast love…"

Success awaits those who steadfastly commit to any requisite sacrifice. **—Ken Poirot**

Reflection Questions

How would you describe the steadfast love of God?

How would you articulate Christ's example of steadfast love?

Do you agree or disagree with this statement: "steadfast love is proven over time, it can't be seen through one singular act."

Why is steadfast love necessary for a successful life in God's eyes?

How is the steadfast love described in this chapter different from how the world would describe steadfast love?

Deeper Study Questions

Read John 13:31-35. Jesus gives a new command that is mentioned in the Old Testament (Leviticus 19). What is new about the command given the greater context of the passage?

With Jesus as the reference point (hint for the previous question), how do we see Jesus living out steadfast love in this passage?

Read 1 John 4:16. What is the love God has for you?

What does it mean to "abide in love"?

Personal Reflections

In the book, I open up as a recipient of steadfast love. Describe a time in your life when you were a recipient of steadfast love.

Of the 7 marks of steadfast love, which most connects with you and why?

"To be successful in steadfast love, you are not looking to be successful for a season. Steadfast love is exemplified over a lifetime." Do you agree? What do you need to do today to begin working towards this?

Challenge

In this book, I talk about a time I was at a conference and the speaker had the audience insert themselves into 1 Corinthians 13. The point was, in short, if Jesus is love, then what is said of love must be true of Jesus. In 1 Corinthians 13, Paul gives us a great definition of Biblical love. Therefore, what defines love, defines Jesus as He is love. If we are to walk as Jesus walked, then it must become something that also defines His followers. For this challenge, I want you to insert your name and then walk through a few questions;

______________ *is patient and kind;* ______________ *does not envy or boast;* ________ *(he/ she) is not arrogant or rude.* ________ *(he/ she) does not insist on* ________ *(his/ her) own way;* ________ *(he/she) is not irritable or resentful;* ________ *(he/ she) does not rejoice at wrongdoing, but rejoices with the truth.* ______________ *bears all things, believes all things, hopes all things, endures all things.*

Having inserted your name, where do you feel the strongest? Where do you feel the weakest?

What can you do to grow in your area of weakness?

Here is the challenge: Having identified your area of weakness, find a piece of Scripture to memorize that would help you in that area. Here are some suggestions:

> Patience: Rejoice in hope, be patient in tribulation, be constant in prayer. Romans 12:12
>
> Kindness: Put on then, as God's chosen ones, holy and beloved, compassionate hearts, kindness, humility, meekness, and patience. Colossians 3:12
>
> Irritable: Whoever is slow to anger has great understanding, but he who has a hasty temper exalts folly. Proverbs 14:29
>
> Pride: Humble yourselves before the Lord, and he will exalt you. James 4:10
>
> Rudeness: A fool gives full vent to his spirit, but a wise man quietly holds it back. Proverbs 29:11

Notes

INGREDIENT #1: STEADFAST LOVE
BIBLICAL CASE STUDY

"Let not steadfast love…"

Turn your tears into joy, stay focused, be steadfast in the storms, (for) they don't last forever. —**Stan the Man**

Reflection Questions

What do you think of when you hear the word steadfast?

What do you think of when you hear the word love?

How do you, now with greater understanding, correlate the two terms?

Why should those who have been wronged desire steadfast love from the offender?

What do you think of this quote, "to want revival without the desire to change, is to not want revival in the first place"?

Deeper Study Questions

Read Hosea 6:1-6. Why didn't God appreciate the people's response?

Why do you think He desires steadfast love?

How did their response not show steadfast love?

Read 1 John 4:7-21. Why is it critical for us to understand the steadfast love of the Lord towards us so we can respond to Him with steadfast love?

Personal Reflections

In what ways do we, in our broken nature, try to show God love in ways He does not find loving?

Who in your life is a great example of steadfast love? What can you learn from their example?

How has God shown you steadfast love?

From what you've learned about steadfast love, where do you need to change how you're loving God or how could you begin showing God steadfast love?

Challenge

Here is my challenge to you for this chapter. We must know the steadfast love of God to display steadfast love back towards God. My challenge to you this week is to read the Gospel of John. As you read, I want you to make note of how John writes about love, how Jesus displays love, and what Jesus teaches about love. The goal is, "Lord, I have failed to love you well, how can I love you better?" We don't dictate loving terms to God; He dictates the terms. I believe as you take time to read the Gospel of John, how He desires to be loved will become clear.

What do you notice about love as you read John's Gospel?

Being in a place where we are no longer dictating terms to God, how do you believe God would want you to love Him moving forward?

Notes

INGREDIENT #2: FAITHFULNESS

"Let not steadfast love and faithfulness forsake you;"

Faithfulness knows no difference between small and great duties. **—John Ruskin**

Reflection Questions

What do you think of when you think of a "faithful person"?

What comes to mind when you think of a "faithful God"?

What most stood out to you about 'faithfulness' from this chapter?

In the reading, I connect faithfulness to God with faithfulness to His mission - why is this a needed connection? How do you see this as a missing connection among many Christians?

Deeper Study Questions

Read Exodus 20:1-21. How does God's faithfulness precede the giving of the Ten Commandments?

Why does God remind the people of His faithfulness before giving the Ten Commandments?

Why is God jealous of our faithfulness?

Read Joshua 21:45 and Psalm 33:4. If a friend questioned the truth of these verses to you, how would you defend the faithfulness of God as described here?

Personal Reflections

In our reading, I said, "In our broken fallen nature, we think ourselves more faithful than we are, and we think the Faithful One to be less faithful than He is." How have you seen this play out in your life?

Which of the seven marks do you feel the strongest in? How so?

Which of the seven marks do you feel the weakest in? Why do you feel this way?

How have you personally experienced the faithfulness of God?

In this book, I referenced a saying from General Jim Mattis, "brilliant in the basics." What is a basic step you can take towards greater faithfulness to God?

Challenge

Over the next few weeks, do two audits of your life: time and money. I think sometimes we think of ourselves more faithful than we are. This week, I want us all to know what we are truly working with. I want us to examine our lives to see our baseline of faithfulness.

For time, track how you spend your time in 15-minutes increments for seven full and consecutive days.

For money, I want you to do two things. First, track your money for a full week. Get a pen and a piece of paper (go old school!) and write down every single expense. In addition, look over your taxes last year and get two numbers: how much you made and how much you recorded for "charitable donations."

After doing this for seven days, come back here and answer these questions:

After tracking your time, what was most eye-opening for you? Have any of your self-perceptions changed?

What might God feel about the way you spend your time?

How can you show greater faithfulness in regard to your time towards God?

After tracking your money and grabbing those numbers from your taxes last year, what was most eye-opening for you? Have any of your self-perceptions changed?

What might God be feeling about the way you spend your money?

How can you show greater faithfulness towards God in regard to how you spend your money?

Notes

INGREDIENT #2: FAITHFULNESS BIBLICAL CASE STUDY

"Let not steadfast love and faithfulness forsake you;"

Well done is better than well said. **—Tom Brady, Sr.**

Reflection Questions

How are "faithfulness" and "success" related terms? How are they unrelated?

At the beginning of the chapter this is said:

> When my life crosses that final finish line, I do not hope to hear, "Well done, good and ***successful*** servant." I have never dreamed of hearing those words from God Almighty. I live like I'm striving to hear those words though. So what do I dream of hearing? "Well done, good and faithful servant." Lord Jesus, this is indeed what I strive to hear.

What are your thoughts on this quote?

Biblically, how would you describe the term "faithful"?

How has "cancel culture" impacted spiritually faithful individuals?

What is it about human nature that allows social influences to influence our spiritual faithfulness?

Deeper Study Questions

Read Genesis 1:1-10. What does this section declare about God? What does it say about God's control of nature?

Here are some crazy things from the Bible: a donkey speaks to a man, seas are parted, a flood takes over the world, the sun stops moving, people walk on water, the land is dry when those seas are parted, and best of all, a dead Man rose from the grave. How does the power mentioned at the start of the Bible help us with the stories that unfold in the rest of the Bible?

Think through Daniel 6. Why does jealousy lead to evil, scheming, and manipulation?

Describe Daniel's faithful character. How did his reputation precede him?

Describe Daniel's faithful actions. In Daniel 6, how did Daniel prove faithful?

Putting it all together, using Daniel as a reference point, what does a faithful man look like?

Lastly, describe the faithfulness of God as seen in Daniel 6.

Personal Reflections

"What would it look like to live a faithful life, not just a few faithful moments?" How would you answer this question in the context of your life?

In Daniel 6, Daniel had a faithful reputation to the point where jealous people had to play his faith to try and silence him. If someone had to play your faith to silence you, could they? How so?

What is the reputation that precedes you? How would people describe you? If you need help, go on social media and post "describe me in three words or less." (Take note of what is said and what is *not* said).

Where in your life is spiritual faithfulness lacking? What does faithfulness towards God look like in that area?

Challenge

In this workbook, you have identified areas of growth. You have had times of reflection, you have done audits, and you have memorized scriptures in relation to your shortcomings. Here is my challenge, right now predetermine faithful steps. Said differently, take the decision out of decision-making.

We all have multiple areas in our lives lacking spiritual faithfulness. What area do you want to focus on for this challenge?

What would greater faithfulness look like in this area?

What decision can you make right now (something you can determine and/or set up) that would guide greater faithfulness in this area?

> I.e., I won't have sex before marriage. When asked, nope, I've already made this decision.
>
> I.e., 2,000 calories is faithful eating. I'm at 1900 calories today; should I have a 600 calories piece of cake? Nope, I've already determined it.
>
> I.e., How do I honor God with finances? I've predetermined to give Him first fruits FIRST at a given percentage. I set up a recurring gift with my church on payday for 10% of my income.

Lastly, do two things: First, tell someone, inviting them to check in on you; Secondly, commit yourself to God in this area.

Whom did you tell? Were you honest and truthful?

Capture a portion of your prayer to God here:

Notes

INGREDIENT #3: COMMITMENT

"Let not steadfast love and faithfulness forsake you;
bind them around your neck"

You need to make a commitment, and once you make it,
then life will give you some answers. **—Les Brown**

Reflection Questions

Is God committed? How would you defend your answer biblically?

What are the similarities and differences between commitment as described by the bible and commitment as lived out by the world?

Do you agree or disagree that "Lacking faith leads to sinking commitment"? Defend your answer.

Before getting into the example of commitment in Daniel 3 (our next section), what are other examples of commitment in the Bible? How do these examples speak to commitment?

Based on how you have answered the previous questions and the 7 marks listed in this chapter, how would you describe a biblically committed person?

Deeper Study Questions

Read Hebrews 10:19-25. How would you describe, from these verses, the faithfulness of God?

In what ways should a Christian's understanding of God's faithfulness lead to greater personal faithfulness?

Read Isaiah 26:3-4

> How is God trustworthy?
>
> How does one keep his or her mind on God?
>
> How does a mind set on God lead to peace in the midst of situations that seem to lack peace?
>
> How do unsettling situations, situations that *naturally* lack peace, tend to test our faith?
>
> How does a focus on God not only aid our peace but also aid our faithfulness?

Personal Reflections

Which of the 7 marks comes easiest to you? Which is the hardest for you? How so?

If you could be great at one thing, what would it be?

What would need to change about your commitments in other (good) areas for you to become great in the area you just wrote down?

How do your personal feelings get in the way of your commitment to God and His mission?

Challenge

Here is my challenge to you: say no to a good thing. Right now, today, quit something. Going into this year, as an example, I had a streak on Duolingo (a language learning app) of over 400 days. I was extremely committed to learning through this app. It became an addiction and something I stressed about daily. In order for me to do what I wanted and needed to do this year, I had to let the streak die. I quit the app so I could be more committed to other areas of my life.

Make a list of everything you are committed to at any level.

What is one area that lacks "great" commitment that God is calling you to give "great" commitment to?

What good commitments are keeping you from being great in that area?

What good thing do you need to quit and/or say no to?

Do it and then circle back here. How did it go? How has this helped your commitment in the area you needed deeper commitment?

Notes

INGREDIENT #3: COMMITMENT BIBLICAL CASE STUDY

"Let not steadfast love and faithfulness forsake you; bind them around your neck"

Integrity is keeping a commitment even after circumstances have changed. **—David Jeremiah**

Reflection Questions

In everyday life, (sports, music, acting, etc.) what is an example of a commitment that stands out to you?

The following is said in the opening paragraph of the chapter; "*You and I wake up each morning with the same battle, it is a battle of wills. Whose will is going to win the day? Yours or God's? To allow God's heart and God's ways to become my ways and my heart, it will require you to be perpetually undone.*" What are your thoughts on this statement?

Do you agree or disagree with the following statement? And why? "When we compare ourselves to the world, we will always walk away with an overinflated view of our commitment and integrity. Is the world the bar? Has it ever been the bar? Christ is the bar. We do not strive to be slightly above average; we strive to be like Christ. This is why a life of full integrity and full commitment to Christ is increasingly rare."

Deeper Study Questions

The Hebrew men faced enormous pressure to conform. How does our culture pressure believers to reject God and conform to the status quo?

Why is it often too late to develop our convictions in the moment of truth? The moment of adversity?

When God doesn't deliver us from dangers, trials, disease, or even death, does that mean He has abandoned us? Why or why not? (*** think about how they respond to the king in Daniel 3:17-18)

Read Romans 12:1-2 Has our life truly been offered up as a living sacrifice? In what ways, yes? In what ways, no?

Read Luke 17:7-10. How does this speak to commitment in Christ's eyes? In a world given to comfort, convenience, ease, and emotions, how does this speak against this? Why are we content giving God our last fruits (leftovers) when He deserves our first fruits?

Read Luke 14:25-35. How does this speak to commitment? How does this challenge your commitment? Where might you need to improve your commitment?

Personal Reflections

This is a powerful story of three young men standing firm. I heard it was once said that depth is not found in interpretation; rather in one's application. Before digging in, what applications to your personal life based on Daniel 3 would cause you to go deeper?

What tests your commitment?

What are some of the idols of our day that vie for your worship?

When has your level of commitment to a cause spoken positively to the people around you? How did it have a positive effect on them?

Think through how you answered the questions from the first section. Take a moment to do an honest inventory of your life and identify an area you feel committed to, yet before God, you have to honestly say you lack commitment.

Challenge

This is a challenge that comes from deep personal reflection. I can be an extreme person. I am deeply committed to causes. At the same time, I am great at hiding and appearing more committed than I really am. A routine area in which I do this is my physical health. I will sneak snacks, not track certain foods in my calorie app, etc. Then I become afraid to step on the scale because I know it will display my lack of commitment. To go spiritual, it will show how I have not honored God with my body.

So, here is the challenge I need to take that I am inviting you to take: identify a metric that will help you gauge your commitment level and tell someone routinely for accountability. That is a mouthful so allow me to illustrate. My metric is the scale. It will clearly show me if I am honoring God with my body. My best friend is Graeme, and he will hold me accountable. Today at lunch, I will tell him of this challenge and ask him to check in on my weight routinely.

What is the metric you need to measure your commitment against?

Whom can you tell to hold you accountable?

What are your bad habits in this area leading to poor commitment? Tell this to the above person as well.

Notes

INGREDIENT #4: HEART

Let not steadfast love and faithfulness forsake you;
bind them around your neck; write them on the
tablet of your heart.

God sees hearts as we see faces. **—George Herbert**

Reflection Questions

What distinguishes two people doing the same thing with a different heart?

What makes a good heart? How would you describe someone with a good heart?

What makes a heart bad? How would you describe someone with a bad heart?

In this chapter, I said, "You can look like a new creation without being a new creation. This is the most important ingredient in the whole recipe. We do our religious acts of love but without a new heart, we are still filthy. We can act religiously faithful, but without a new heart, we are still filthy. We can be religiously committed, but without a new heart, we are still filthy." Do you agree or disagree? Why?

Deeper Study Questions

"The heart is deceitful above all things, and desperately sick; who can understand it?" (Jeremiah 17:9). What does this say about the natural condition of the human heart?

Read Matthew 15:1-9. Culturally speaking, the Pharisees appeared to be among the holiest in society. How did Jesus see them, examining them to their heart?

Read Isaiah 64:6. Why does God see our good as filthy if we do not have a new heart?

Read 2 Corinthians 5:16-21. Describe how one, through Jesus, experiences heart change.

With that verse still in mind, as ambassadors with a new heart, what are we to do as new creations?

Personal Reflections

I was open when I said of myself, "As a fleshly Pharisee, I battle a judgmental and condemning spirit. As a fleshly Pharisee, my sin is 'better' than others' sin. As a fleshly Pharisee, I have learned how to look good without being good." Can you relate? How so?

Which of the seven marks comes easiest to you? Why?

Which of the seven marks come hardest to you? Why?

How did Jesus' example in John 4 impact you?

How would you describe the heart issue behind your most common sins?

If Jesus had complete control of your heart, what would change about you?

Challenge

I just asked you to think about the heart issue behind your sin. Before I challenge you, read Matthew 15:10-20. Sin flows out of the heart. I am a glutton by nature. I stress eat and overeat when I am bored. In both cases, I take my eyes off Jesus. In both cases, I look to food to provide instead of my actual Provider. Psalm 119 mentions we are to hide God's word in our hearts so that we will not sin against Him. I want us to be holy before God. Memorizing scripture helps us do so. So a few questions than the challenge.

What are the repeated sins in your life? Why do you repeat them?

What lies do you tend to believe amid that sin?

What truth about God would help you dispose of those lies?

With the chapter, the questions from this section, and your experience in mind, what is the heart issue behind your sin?

The challenge: identify scripture dealing with the heart issue you struggle with and then put that scripture to memory.

Common heart issues with scripture: (not an exhaustive list)

Anxiety: 1 Peter 5:7

Fear: Isaiah 41:10

Distrust: Psalm 13:5

Control: Proverbs 25:28

Jealousy: James 3:16-17

Envy: Ecclesiastes 4:4

Unforgiveness: Colossians 3:13

Ungrateful: Romans 1:21

Notes

INGREDIENT #4: HEART
BIBLICAL CASE STUDY

Let not steadfast love and faithfulness forsake you;
bind them around your neck; write them on
the tablet of your heart.

We know the truth, not only by the reason
but also by the heart. **—Blaise Pascal**

Reflection Questions

How would you describe a person's non-physiological heart?

Do you agree or disagree with this quote: "There is no failure like moral failures. There is no failure like sin failure." Explain why.

We've seen many people tweet or hold news conferences after being outed for a wrong. What is the best example of someone taking ownership of their wrong that you can remember? What is the worst?

Biblical success is when God's heart and God's ways become my heart and my way. How can an unsuccessful life do the things of God without the heart of God?

What are the differences between shame and sorrow?

What are the differences between discipline and condemnation?

Why is an understanding of the difference between these four words important for us as it relates to a heart response out of failure?

Deeper Study Questions

Read 1 Samuel 13:14, 1 Samuel 16:7, 1 Kings 11:4, and Acts 13:22. How would you describe David based on these verses?

What did David do leading up to Psalm 51? How would you describe his moral failure? (2 Samuel 11)

Read Psalm 51: What does this Psalm communicate about the heart of God:

1. Towards sin?
2. Towards the sinner?
3. Towards the process of restoration?

What does it mean to be contrite, broken, and sorrowful over our sins?

Read Proverbs 28:13. Why is it important that we confess our sins to those we have wronged?

Personal Reflections

Read Matthew 5:21-30. If we are honest with ourselves, how are we able to relate to David in his sin?

How do you typically respond to failure?

Describe a time you responded well to failure.

Describe a time you responded poorly to failure.

What role does confession of sin play in your life? What role should it play?

Read Romans 8:1-8 and Romans 8:31-39. How does this help you to know Christ's heart as you approach Him with the confession of sin?

Challenge

Here is the challenge: write your psalm (prayer) as a confession of sin. ***note: your psalm is not biblical, as the Bible is complete. It is, however, personal.

Some questions to help guide and then space to write out a psalm (prayer) to God…

What is the sin you need to confess to God?

What do you know of God that should guide your prayer?

How does God feel about your sin?

How does He feel about you?

What do you feel about your sin?

What do you feel about God?

What do you need to commit to moving forward?

Now write your psalm prayer with all these elements (the above questions) included…

Notes

RESULT #1: FAVOR
BIBLICAL CASE STUDY

Let not steadfast love and faithfulness forsake you; bind them around your neck; write them on the tablet of your heart. So you will find favor..."

Grace is the overflowing favor of God, and you can always count on it being available to draw upon as needed. **—Oswald Chambers**

Reflection Questions

Section one, the recipe, teaches us how to live life in God's ways with His heart. If someone is truly excelling in steadfast love, faithfulness, commitment, and cultivating the right heart, what would you expect the result of their lives to be?

How did the case study on Noah shape your understanding of Biblical favor?

What is your reaction to this quote? *"We think if we do X, God will do Y. But is God's favor really a math equation? Is it really tit for tat? That sounds more like religion than a relationship. Give enough and I'll get enough. Read enough and God will do this for me. Pray enough and I'll get the job."*

What is your reaction to this paragraph from the book?

> Mary was favored, was she not? The angel said, "o favored one." (Luke 1:28). What did God's favor lead to? Pain. Living with the reputation, in a very religious culture, of being sexually disobedient. How did that religious culture treat people with a sinful reputation? Terribly. She likely lost her husband Joseph during Jesus' childhood. What would it have been like to be widowed with a sexually sinful reputation in Israel during biblical times? Terrible. She was there to see her Son die a brutal death on a cross. Can you imagine? But she was favored. She, unlike any other mother on earth, helped raise a truly perfect Son. She found God's favor and lived a faithful life to the end.

Deeper Study Questions

Read Gen. 6:5-9. What is said about Noah that is "favorable?" How does one live like this?

How does this description of Noah fit the "recipe" we have spoken about in the first section?

What did God's favor of Noah lead to?

Read Luke 1:26-28. What did Mary's favored position lead to? What hardship would she face as a result of this?

Both Mary and Noah experienced both privilege and hardship. What do you make of this when it comes to being favored by God?

God's favor did not happen in isolation, there was favor for a purpose. With this in mind, what is God's favor meant to accomplish?

How does this conversation differ from the prosperity gospel?

Personal Reflections

When has God's favor annoyed you? (Perhaps in someone else)

With a new understanding of God's favor, where might God be showing you favor that you had not previously seen?

With a Biblical understanding of favor, why is favor easy to miss in our own lives?

When was a time you looked to God with a prosperity gospel, a worldly understanding of favor? How did this faulty understanding impact how you viewed God?

Challenge

One of the points we make in this chapter is that God's favor is to put you on a mission. God shows favor to enable us to attack what He would like us to attack. So this challenge is a "build your own challenge." Here, I want you to identify where God is showing you favor and then challenge yourself to build God's kingdom through His favor.

Where is God showing you favor?

How can God's favor be seen as a resource to build His kingdom?

First, pause and pray, "God, in light of your favor, how do you want me to build your kingdom?" Pray this with a spirit of "thy will be done." Do not assume the heart of God; pray for understanding of the heart of God. So now, having paused to pray, how might God want you to build His kingdom based on His favor in your life?

In light of how you have answered these questions, write out a succinct challenge for yourself and a plan to make it happen.

Notes

RESULT #2: SUCCESS WITH GOD BIBLICAL CASE STUDY

Let not steadfast love and faithfulness forsake you;
bind them around your neck; write them on the tablet
of your heart. So you will find favor and good
success in the sight of God…"

Our greatest fear should not be of failure but of succeeding at things in life that don't really matter. **—Francis Chan**

Reflection Questions

In what ways is the definition of a successful life different between the world and as defined by God?

What is success?

"If you understand truth, wisdom or foolishness is on full display in your response. How you respond to stated truth will define you as a fool or wise person." Do you agree or disagree and why?

The chapter drove us to this main point; "abundance awaits the faithful!" Out of context, this seems like the prosperity gospel. Within the context, what is meant by this statement?

What would it be like to stand before God having never been used by Him to lead someone to the saving knowledge of Jesus Christ?

Deeper Study Questions

Read Matthew 25:14-30. What is the difference between the servants who multiplied their talent and the one who didn't?

From a human perspective, what is risky about what the multipliers did? Why do you think Christ rewards this behavior?

What makes human sense about what the one talent servant did? Why do you think Christ sees this as worthless?

Practically speaking, how does the reality of eternal punishment affect how you live day to day?

How does this passage speak to the glory of Jesus Christ?

Personal Reflections

What fruit is being produced in your life in correlation with the truth you know of God? (Identify the fruit and the correlating truth; IE: I give 10% of my income because I know God is the Provider)

Where might God look at your life and think "fruitless"?

Based on your above answer, what is the lie you are believing about God, the doubt you are accepting or the misguided perspective of God you are living in?

Where are you playing it safe where God might want you to start investing your God-given talents?

Why do we tend to think playing it safe is wise? How should you move forward being risky for Jesus without being a biblical fool?

Jesus will come back suddenly, and we will have to give an account. How can we multiply the talents He's given us to build the kingdom?

Challenge

Head over to Google and type in "Spiritual gift assessment." The challenge is to take two spiritual gifts assessments and then do something about them to build the kingdom of God!

Where did you find agreement between the two spiritual gifts assessments? What are your spiritual gifts?

Search Google for a greater understanding of your spiritual gift. After taking time to understand it better, how does a Christian's faithfulness with your spiritual gift help build God's kingdom?

Now, send an email to the pastoral staff at church. Let them know what your spiritual gift is and ask them how you could utilize this gift through the local church. What did they say?

If you get no response, or you are not satisfied with their response, what will you do about it? How will you be faithful with the talent God has given you?

Notes

RESULT #3: SUCCESS WITH MAN
BIBLICAL CASE STUDY

Let not steadfast love and faithfulness forsake you; bind them around your neck; write them on the tablet of your heart. So you will find favor and good success in the sight of God and man."

It is not your business to succeed, but to do right: when you have done so, the rest lies with God. **—C.S. Lewis**

Reflection Questions

How would you describe "success with man?"

Why does pain bring many to a crisis of faith?

"It is hard to stay humble and selfless through pain. Why? Whether it's you or me, I just want this pain to end. Yet, what I hope we will see in this chapter is that the humble don't mumble or grumble through pain. This type of humility leads to success

by God with man." After reading the chapter, what are your thoughts on this quote?

Why do well-meaning Christians give terrible advice in the midst of pain?

Why is it hard to hear what well-meaning people say in the midst of pain?

Why is perspective hard to gain in the midst of pain?

Deeper Study Questions

Describe the challenges in Joseph's life leading up to Genesis 41.

As Joseph sat in a literal jail cell, what would you expect him to be feeling and thinking?

How is faith fortified differently through hardship than through times of blessing?

Why did Joseph say the interpretation of dreams belongs to God? What does that reveal about Joseph's perspective on life, gifting, and faith?

Where do you see evidence of Joseph's humility? How is that humble?

From Prison to Palace, Joseph's story is one of Humiliation to Exaltation. What does this teach us about the pattern of the Christian Life (See 1 Pet. 5:6-7)?

How is this pattern demonstrated in the Life of Christ?

Personal Reflections

What have been the hardest moments in your life?

What moments drew you closer to God?

What are your current hardships?

Whether you are in a time of blessing or hardship, what is God teaching you that is unique to the situation you are in? Or what do you think God is trying to teach you now that you think about it?

How would you respond to the question; "How does humility keep us from grumbling amid hardship?"

Challenge

It is hard to stay anchored to Jesus in the storms of life if we do not have habits to daily connect with Jesus. From the mature to the immature faith, we all have room to improve our time with Jesus. In this challenge, I want you and I to audit our devotional life and take a step to improve it.

What are your daily habits of connecting with Jesus?

Imagine being dead and now standing in the presence of Jesus, read your above answer out loud. In the face of Jesus, what feels insufficient about your answer?

Prayer, bible reading, bible memorization, worship, journaling, (and more) are all parts of an effective devotional life. What area of an effective devotional life do you most need to improve on?

What in life hinders or creates challenges from making time for God a daily aspect of your life?

Who in your life do you feel has an effective and powerful devotional life? Text them now and ask them, "what are your daily habits with Jesus." What stands out to you?

What changes do you need to make in daily habits with Jesus to spend better time with Jesus? How will you put this into immediate practice?

Notes

GOD'S HEART AND GOD'S WAYS IN FAVOR AND SUCCESS

Let not steadfast love and faithfulness forsake you; bind them around your neck; write them on the tablet of your heart. So you will find favor and good success in the sight of God and man."

Those who have failed miserably are often the first to see God's formula for success… **—Erwin Lutzer**

Reflection Questions

We have said, "*Biblical success is when God's heart and God's ways become my heart and my way.*" How would successfully living this out challenge everyday life?

What do you think of this quote? "Following Jesus (part one of this book) will cost you the typical human experience."

Why is it human nature to want to be rewarded when hard work has led to a successful outcome?

In your own words, how would you describe favor, success, and blessing biblically?

Deeper Study Questions

Read Proverbs 30:8-9. How is this an affront to success and favor based on worldly thinking? How would this mindset make us live our lives as God calls us to live?

Read Job 1 and 2. How was Job living a successful life? What did it lead to?

Read Job 42:10-17. What do you make of the way the book of Job ends as it relates to our discussion on favor and success?

Read 1 Thessalonians 5:18. God's favor and success may test us, cost and demand more from us. How does a proper understanding of God's favor and success help us to give thanks in all circumstances?

Read Ephesians 4:13-15 and Colossians 2:6-7.

> In light of these verses and what you have read in this book, how should favor and success grow us towards maturity in Christ?
>
> How did Jesus, our suffering servant, embody success and favor?

Personal Reflections

Which of the seven areas used to describe favor and success most challenged you? Why?

What is an area of your life that seems more successful now that you've read this chapter? How did this chapter help you rethink that area?

When have you experienced success and favor that helped to mature you?

When have you experienced success that weakened your faith?

How can you focus on maturity through success and favor in everyday life?

Challenge

In this book, I mention this Rick Warren's quote, "God is more interested in your character than your comfort. God is more interested in making your life holy than He is in making your life happy." In light of this thinking and the verse we just read from 1 Thessalonians 5:18, here is a simple challenge: express gratitude. It is only simple when devoid of circumstances.

What circumstances in life, humanly speaking, would not elicit feelings of gratitude?

Why is spiritual growth something to be thankful for?

Based on the work you've done in this section and what you have read, express gratitude to God for what is currently going on in your life.

Notes

CONCLUSION

Reflection Questions

What does life all about Jesus look like?

What does life all about people look like?

Look back on your answers to those two questions, what is different and what is similar about your answers?

Deeper Study Questions

Read John 13:31-35. How is this part of a successful life? How does this verse help us to love God and love people?

Read Proverbs 3:3-4. How is this verse simple? How is this verse deep?

Read Proverbs 3:5-6. How does this guide a person forward?

Personal Reflections

Having all but concluded this workbook and having concluded the book itself, what are your three biggest takeaways?

What habits have you already put into practice based on what you have read? How is it going?

What habits do you need to put in place? What is your plan?

Challenge

Psalm 90:12 says, "so teach us to number our days that we may get a heart of wisdom." I looked up the average lifespan and set my retirement date. Cool Jason sounds lame. It is. But every day in my five-year journal, I write out how many days I have left till retirement and death. As of this morning, I have 14,334 days till death and 9,514 till I retire. I want to use my days wisely. It helps to start with the end in mind. In this chapter, I boil my Grandfather's life down to two primary lessons. Here is my challenge: and then a question for you. My challenge, write your eulogy based on the two main things you hope would be said of your life. Think about what success is. Think about what you hope others will see as a successful life. Think about what God sees as a successful life.

Your eulogy:

What do you need to do today to get you to the successful life you hope to live?

Notes

About Kharis Publishing

•

Kharis Publishing, an imprint of Kharis Media LLC, is a leading Christian and inspirational book publisher based in Aurora, Chicago metropolitan area, Illinois. Kharis' dual mission is to give voice to under-represented writers (including women and first-time authors) and equip orphans in developing countries with literacy tools. That is why, for each book sold, the publisher channels some of the proceeds into providing books and computers for orphanages in developing countries so that these kids may learn to read, dream, and grow. For a limited time, Kharis Publishing is accepting unsolicited queries for nonfiction (Christian, self-help, memoirs, business, health, and wellness) from qualified leaders, professionals, pastors, and ministers. Learn more at: About Us - Kharis Publishing - Accepting Manuscript

www.ingramcontent.com/pod-product-compliance
Lightning Source LLC
Chambersburg PA
CBHW060039050426
42448CB00012B/3075
* 9 7 8 1 6 3 7 4 6 4 4 3 4 *